THE CRUCIBLE

A Tale of the Kentucky Feuds

BY

BURNS OF THE MOUNTAINS

Oneida, Ky.

THE ONEIDA INSTITUTE

1928

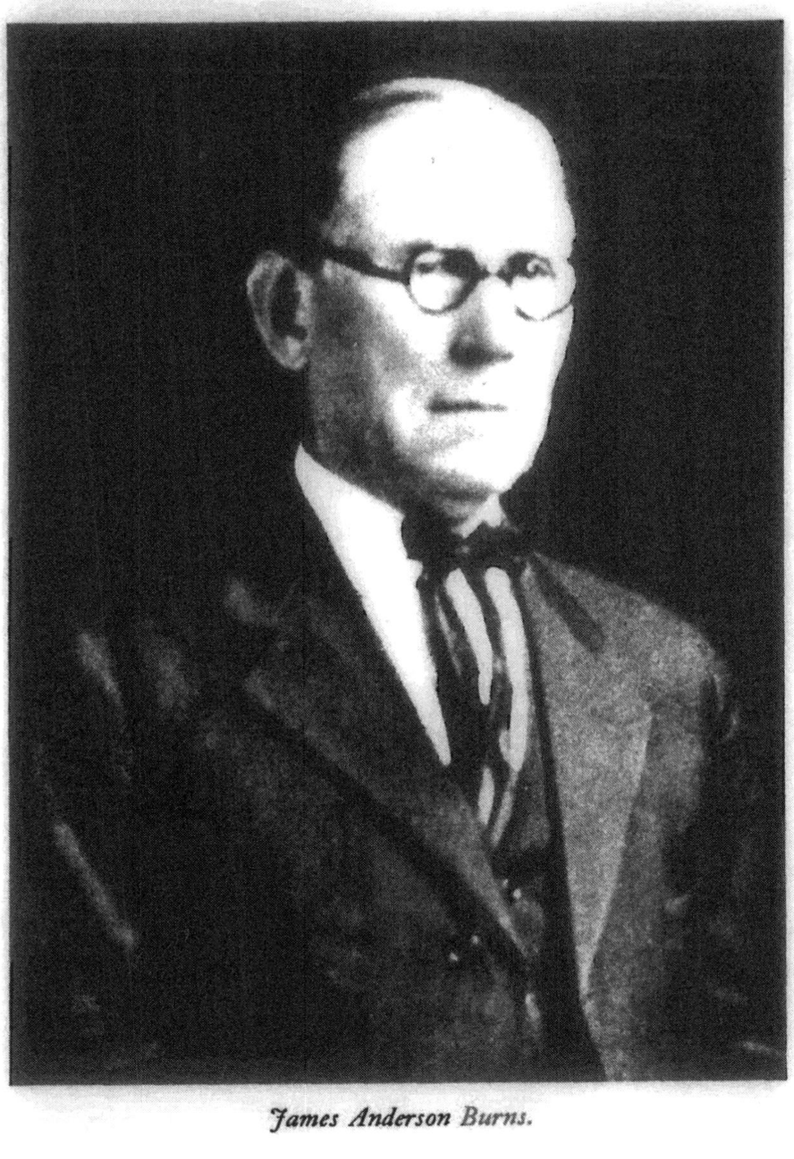

James Anderson Burns.

FROM A HEART FILLED WITH
GRATITUDE, THIS BOOK IS DED-
ICATED TO EVERY FRIEND OF
ONEIDA INSTITUTE, PAST, PRES-
ENT AND FUTURE.

A Prelude

ONE DAY in the midst of the busy life of a great city, the writer, whose honor, in being associated with this book's author and the work he represents, is all too inadequately acknowledged, watched the demolition of a building on one of the world's busy corners. Modern machinery of the latest type for such work was in operation, walls were falling, debris was being handled and removed with machine speed, and soon the corner would know the old structure no more, and even the citizens would allow the memories of the old theatre to fade. Quickly there came to him, the living parable before him—Construction so difficult, Destruction so easy— just as this book tells in its panorama, of the tragic destruction of life in the feuds.

But this book sets in the midst of the facts of destruction and human, tragic suffering, the nobler and heroic and far more profitable herculean efforts of a man with a vision, vim and seemingly inexhaustible vitality. No one will peruse its pages and visualize its scenes, without being commanded and commissioned by its human message. Here is a man speaking from a life that has known abysmal nadirs and heaven-high zeniths. Of his stature, one is not in error, when he says—'Lincolnian.' Of his gifted command of English, not less than Anglo-Saxon in its Kentucky, pristine beauty. Of his life's achievements, inferior and unjust would be the appraisal, that did not designate it—Momentous, Monumental and Munificent. Of his faith, Lowell wrote of such as him, when he indited the lines of "The Present Crisis"—

"Count me o'er life's chosen heroes—

They were souls who stood alone . . . " but yet, that would not be wholly accurate, for his was the faith of Abram, when he left Ur of the Chaldees; of Moses, when he chose "to suffer affliction . . . seeing Him who is invisible"; and of him in the triumph of his faith, exclaimed — "For we know that all things work together for good . . . ."

For 12 and more years the broad expanses of our country have heard his voice (worth a million dollars, in one business man's estimate), from the pulpits of Churches, the platforms of Chautauquas, Educational centres and Lyceum Bureaus, where with ever the same fidelity to the cause, that weighed so upon his heart, through Divine design, he called individuals and organizations into coöperative friendship with the Institution, of which he is both Founder and President.

This volume, the fruitage of his years of thought, faith and labor, goes out to the centres of commerce, to the hamlets of many hillsides, to the ports of plenty, afar and a-near, not simply with a story of an entrancing kind, but with a meaningful message fraught with the stuff that life is made up of.

To have been asked to prepare the prelude for this work is a high honor, I am sensitive to, and in humble effort of simple word and honest conviction and accurate description, some recognition of that fact is here made.

So is launched a compelling character story, A Corsair of The Cumberlands, where men are first *Men* and life is unadorned with the trappings of the artificial. "Burns of the Mountains" calls to the Dwellers by the Seas, Citizens of the Cities and People of the Plains— With A Vision, In A Virile Voice, For Veritable Volunteers.

God Speed Thee—Noble Tale Of A Noble Life!

ROBERT T. TUMBLESTON, *Pastor*

Lower Dublin Baptist Church, Phila., Pa.

"Fetch your chairs and come on."
It was the only home I had.

CHAPTER I.

MY BOYHOOD home, high up on a mountain in West Virginia, was a log-cabin—indispensably a log cabin for reasons, not sentimental, but purely economic. No other kind of building would have been possible at that time and in that place.

The logs were cut from the roundest, straightest and most accessible trees of the proper size in the surrounding forest. Many different kinds were used—oak, hickory, ash, poplar, etc. Even the bark was not removed from the logs. They were left exactly as they grew. There was neither time nor money for anything better.

When I was four years old, my father borrowed a broadaxe from a neighbor, hewed out wide puncheons, and laid a floor. Before that, the floor was nothing but earth.

Bumble bees bored holes for their habitations in the soft-wood logs, and Dirt Daubers plastered their adobe homes on the walls. One of the sills was hollow, at one end, and a nest of yellow jackets lived in it for several years.

Many crickets were on the hearth, and under the hearth. They ate holes in our stockings, but we must not kill them. It was the worst kind of bad luck. We must hang our stockings on a pole suspended from one of the joists.

We had very little furniture — all of the crudest homemade kind. Only absolutely necessary things were allowed space between the narrow walls. Eighteen by twenty feet is a small boundary within which to house a family.

I never saw a cooking stove till I was fifteen years old. It was a curious innovation in the home of a neighbor. This radical departure from time-honored custom met with disapproval, and the erring neighbor lost caste to some extent.

My mother had wonderful skill in the use of oldtime cooking utensils — pots, kettles, ovens, etc. When she had placed the frugal meal on the crude puncheon table she would say, "Fetch your chairs and come on." We did.

What a home! Its memories linger and haunt. It was the only home I had.

CHAPTER II.

MY FATHER, Hugh Burns, was the only man I ever knew who actually lived in accord with his convictions.

He raised a plentiful support on his little farm, but he worked with his own hands—not with the hands of others. He hired no work except in harvest. The prices he paid never fluctuated. For work in corn harvest he paid fifty cents a day or one bushel of corn; in wheat harvest, one dollar a day, or one bushel of wheat. In every case the hired man was a member of the family, board and bed free.

There was a very small surplus of corn, wheat, potatoes and bacon, each year, which he sold at the following prices:

One bushel of corn, fifty cents;

One bushel of wheat, one dollar;

One bushel of potatoes, fifty cents;

One pound of bacon, ten cents.

The market prices mattered nothing whatever. His prices never changed. He would sell only one grist (two bushels) of corn to one man. Other neighbors might be in need.

He preached for four widely scattered Primitive Baptist churches — one Sunday each month for each church. One of the churches was forty miles away, the others not so far. He always walked to his meetings. He rendered all this service without a salary. The hireling cared not for the flock.

His home was established on the basis of personal independence.

He raised little patches of cotton and flax each year. I can vividly picture the flax break, the hackle, the cards, the spinning-wheels, the loom, the tan trough, the shoemaker's bench, and the oldtime hand mill. These things are still a part of my being—inescapable.

I never heard him express a political opinion. He never went to an election. His only part in civic affairs was to obey the laws. Evidently, he belonged to a kingdom not of this world.

But he was rich in the friendship of all who knew him. Did he solve the problem of life? Who can say?

Our Library consisted of only four books and an almanac—but each was a classic.

CHAPTER III.

OUR library consisted of four books—a Bible, Thomas' Hymns, Pilgrims Progress, and Josephus. Where and how we got them I do not know. They were right there as long ago as I can remember.

Besides these, we had a new Almanac each year. It was full of Signs of the Zodiac, Conjectures of the Weather, Eclipses, Josh Billings' Yarns, and scores of Testimonials to the Miraculous Efficacy of Hostetter's Stomach Bitters.

I learned to read in the Almanac, and almost committed the other four books to memory.

This course of study was carried on at night, by the light of the wood fire, on rainy days and Sundays, and in winter when the weather was too cold for work.

There were no instructors except the dusky shadows in the corners of the cabin, and the whispering silences all around.

My father, as he sat before the fire and slowly combed his beard, would often say, "Jim, I can never give you an education. I have no money. But I do want to teach you this: 'never accept anything you do not earn.'"

This oft-repeated precept did not impress me very

much at the time. But in after years I came to regard it as the greatest thing in my education.

In all, I have had seventeen months of actual schooling — about twelve months in the Public Schools in West Virginia, and one semester in Dennison University.

But in the early days I formed the habit of studying by myself. And, throughout the years, I have studied events and books and men first-hand — not always by the firelight, but always with this potent precept ringing in my ears: "Never accept anything you do not earn."

CHAPTER IV.

They are building a new school house down at the 'Perry Field.'"

This announcement was made by my brother Robert who had just returned from Newton. The "Perry Field," an old waste place, was three and one half miles away.

I was filled with wonder. I had never seen a school house. The nearest one was at Newton, a distance of eight miles from our home.

I went down to the "Perry Field" early the next day. Sure enough, the workmen were laying the foundation. I was elated. My fondest dream was coming true. At last, at the age of fourteen, I was to be a school boy.

The next thing was school books. But how was I to get them? I decided in favor of the "Sang (Ginseng) hoe."

Accordingly, I took to the woods, armed with "Sang hoe" and "Sang bag." Every day that could be spared from the growing crop was employed in arduous searchings for this lucrative plant.

The plants were few and far between. They grew in secluded jungles in rich coves and hollows. The finding of a dozen plants was a good day's work. The roots of

The first plank house I ever saw.

fifty plants, when dried, would weigh one pound—worth two dollars in the market.

These "Sanging" trips always led in the direction of the "Perry Field." I could "Sang" through the mountains to the new school house, inspect it, and then "Sang" back home.

The new school house was finished in due time. It was a beautiful little white building trimmed in brown —the first plank house I ever saw. Then there was a week of anxious waiting for school to begin.

The day before dawned at last, and my father rode away to Newton with the precious package of "Sang." He returned late in the afternoon with the more precious package of books, and my first pair of "store shoes."

In the package I found McGuffey's Speller, McGuffey's Third Reader, Mitchell's Geography, Harvey's Grammar, and Ray's Practical Arithmetic.

I examined them carefully. I placed them on the table in a neat pile. I gazed at them lovingly for a long time. Then I said, "Daddy, I must learn everything in these books." It was the happiest moment of my life.

At the age of sixteen, I had completed the Curriculum of the Common Schools. I had also seen visions of a big, busy world stretching far beyond the confines of our mountain barriers. My soul yearned to go. But whither?

I had often heard my parents talking, in guarded tones, of the old Kentucky home and the Blood Feuds of the Cumberlands—usually after they had retired at night. This led me to think of Kentucky as a land of mystery, romance and opportunity. I would go there.

But there were two questions which had fastened themselves on my mind—perplexing questions. These must be answered and then I would go.

To this end, I sought my father with considerable trepidation. He was just a little bit inaccessible—not a man to be questioned lightly.

*In the days of long ago a boy's only
hope for books or a pair of store shoes
was the "Sang hoe."*

CHAPTER V

Daddy, why did you leave Kentucky?"

"Now what do you want to know that for?"

"I think it is fair that I should know. Tell me."

"Well, if you must know, I left Kentucky to get away from the feuds."

"What are feuds, Daddy?"

"Oh, you can't understand! Why are you asking these questions, anyhow?"

"Daddy, I can understand. I can understand anything you tell me, and I want to know——now."

"All right then. A feud is a mutual, deadly hatred between families."

"What do you mean by deadly hatred?"

"I mean that they had killed our loved ones and that we hated them for it——would wreak vengeance without extenuation or mercy. Then they would wreak vengeance upon us just the same."

"How did the feuds get started?"

"Well, it was long before I was born, before my father was born. They say there were two boys who loved the same girl. Serious trouble ensued. The girl mother hung herself. The two boys locked themselves in a room and killed each other with knives. Reprisals in

I left Kentucky to get away from the feuds.

life were made, and the trouble spread and grew."

: "In what way did it spread and grow?"

"Why, they told it to their children and to their children's children in their cradles. In this way, the deadly hatred grew and spread from family to family and from generation to generation."

"Was our family involved?"

"All the mountain families were involved."

"Some of our people were killed?"

"Many of them."

"And you left them to fight the battle alone?"

"I didn't run away from the fight. I left to save my boys from inevitable slaughter."

"I am sorry you left, Daddy—more sorry than I can tell you."

"Jim, you are mad, and your thoughts are evil. When a man is mad all his thoughts, words and acts are evil."

"Daddy, I am going to Kentucky."

He looked at me for several seconds, a strange light burning in his deep brown eyes (was it the light of long-slumbering battle fires?), then calmly said, "You are not going to Kentucky—now. You will get mixed up in the feuds."

"I shall do exactly what I think is right."

"Every way of a man is right in his own eyes, Jim."

"Daddy, I am going. Nothing anyone can say or do shall prevent me. I—am—going."

The Old Burns Homestead

Again he looked at me, piercingly, as though he would search my very soul. Then he turned away, sighed deeply, gazed into the fire, and began slowly combing his beard.

I knew that he had reached a decision. But I knew, also, that his decision was a sealed book for the present. The seance was ended.

CHAPTER VI.

THE next evening I found him sitting under the cherry tree in our yard. Now I would ask the other question.

"Daddy, why do you and Bill argue so much?"

"I never argue with him at all. He always argues with me, and I don't know why he does it."

"But why do you belong to different churches? You are both preachers, and your Bibles are exactly alike."

"Well, when I was converted I found that I loved the fellowship of people who believed that God is almighty, that He does all His will continually both in heaven and earth. I found such people in the Primitive Baptist churches. So I joined with them."

"But does not Bill believe in the same God?"

"Sometimes I think he does. Most of the time he seems to believe in some kind of a god who, in creating the world, involved himself in a difficulty from which he has never been able to extricate either himself or the people he created."

"But, Daddy, does not Bill read the same Bible which you read? How do you account for such absolutely conflicting interpretations?"

"Jim, some day you will learn that the Bible means

26

to a man just what his heart wants it to mean—nothing more, nothing less."

Again he sighed, took his little comb from his pocket, and slowly combed his beard. That was the end. He had spoken.

For an hour, or maybe more, I sat on the edge of the porch and gazed at the stars, trying to grasp the meaning of those strange words of his which each seemed to weigh a pound or more.

In the arguments, I had always sided with my brother Bill. But, in answering my questions, he had punctured my armor. I was wounded. Little did I dream that those few, simple words of his should exert such a tremendous influence in determining the very foundations of my life work.

CHAPTER VII

Sɪʟᴇɴᴄᴇ reigned for a week. It was Friday morning. My father was starting to one of his churches in Kanawha County. I walked with him to the edge of the woods.

Suddenly he stopped and said, "Jim, you are planning to leave home while I am gone." I hung my head in guilty silence. How had he guessed my intentions?

Seeing my confusion, he placed his hand on my shoulder and continued, "I want you to promise me that you will not go to Kentucky till next year. If you will put it off till then, your mother and I will go with you. You are all I have left. The rest have homes of their own. I would be very lonely if you should go so far away. Will you promise this—for me?"

"Yes—for you—I will promise this."

His grip on my shoulder tightened. It was a caress. He stood thus, looking into my eyes for a few seconds, then turned away and, with swinging stride, faced his walk of forty miles—his last long walk.

Late on Monday afternoon, a neighbor came to me where I was plowing on the hillside and said, "Your father died last night—heart failure."

Bill, Rob and I went and buried him but it has never

Facing his walk of forty miles. His last long walk.

seemed to me that the lifeless thing, which we lowered into the grave, was my father. I have never been able to realize that he is dead but, rather, that he has gone away for awhile.

CHAPTER VIII.

THE next year, faithful to my promise, I took my mother to Kentucky—to the old "Burns Homestead," at the forks of Bull Skin, forty miles from the nearest railroad.

Here I found a peculiar country, about fifteen thousand square miles of it, called, "The Mountains." The homes, strangely like my father's in architecture, lay low in the valleys, on the banks of the creeks and the little rivers, while above them, vastly rich in undeveloped resources of coal and timber, the towering Cumberlands lifted their majestic peaks into the azure of sunny southern skies.

Here, also, I found a peculiar people (five hundred thousand of them), the direct, unadulterated descendants of the early colonists, with scarcely a drop of alien blood in their veins. They had been shut in here (held in abeyance) by mountain barriers for more than a century—a little empire of their own.

Few, if any, were educated. Nearly all were illiterate. But they represented a high degree of intelligence. They were intensely religious and patriotic. Seventy-five percent of them were Baptists of one kind or another, and about the same percentage were Republicans —"Stand-patters."

First Home of Burns of the Mountains.

They knew the salient points of history, Ancient Medieval, and Modern. They were well versed in the dogmas of Theology. They had in tradition what the world had in books. They had told it to their children and to their children's children throughout the generations.

They knew scores of the old hymns "by heart." They sang many of the old ballads—Brennon on the Moor, Fair Eleanor, Barbara Allen, and such like.

I sometimes found books (old classics) in homes where no inmate had been able to read for a hundred years. Evidently they had retrograded in some things. But they still maintained the University of the Fireside.

Their standards of manhood were remarkably high. If a man tried to shirk the payment of an honest debt, he was a "rascal." If he was a moral libertine, he was "low down." If he was a coward, "the dogs wouldn't bark at him." If he was a drunkard, he was "nobody." No matter what his financial condition might be, if he was brave, honest, honorable and "hard-working" he was an honored member of the highest caste.

CHAPTER IX.

PRACTICALLY all of them were involved in the feuds, just as my father had said. But on this subject they were quite reticent. When I alluded to the feuds, in any way, they fell into a silence which was painful. The Feud Spirit pervaded the whole atmosphere. There were shadows on the hearth and skeletons in the closet —things of which they did not talk to strangers.

But I waited patiently, and they soon took me into their confidence — admitted me into their councils. They had adopted me, although no word to that end was spoken, no pledge of any kind proposed. I was one of them. A cousin, some years older, made me a present of a heavy pistol and said, "You might need this sometime. You understand?" I understood very well.

One afternoon as I walked down a lonely path, skirted by a fringe of tall iron weeds, I heard a tense, angry voice demanding, "Stop right where you are! Don't you come another step! Drop that pistol! You killed my brother for nothing! Stop, you murdering dog! You are only half a second from H—!"

A shot rang out—more shots.

I stepped through the patch of weeds and there stood

A feudist in the making.
"This is the coat he wore that day."

a lad, about fifteen years old, deliberately firing into a beech tree.

"What are you doing?" I asked.

He came slowly to me, confused but smiling, the smoking weapon in his hand, and said, "I was trying out my new pistol. She is dead centre."

But I knew that he was training for the fight which must come sooner or later—inuring himself to bloodshed. The day of pitiless vengeance would surely dawn and then he must be calm, deliberate, skillful, relentless—maintain the age-old honor of his clan.

A few days after this I visited one of my relatives, a widow.

In words of burning eloquence, she told me the heart-rending story of her husband's death. Then she went to the rusty old bureau, took out a homespun coat, pointed to the bullet holes and the dark stains, and said in pitiful tones, "This is the coat he wore that day."

A bright, manly boy of twelve stood by and watched his mother's tears mingle with the blood stains on his dead father's coat. His bosom heaved. His eyes flashed forth the unmistakable battle light.

It was very easy to understand. It was so primitive, so simple, so sincere. That boy's one predominant purpose in life was to avenge that blood and those tears. This mother, unintentionally perhaps, had made a feudist of her little boy. This—fostering hatred in infant hearts—is the efficient cause of Mountain Vendettas and of World Wars—just the same.

I shall never forget the first feud-battle which I witnessed. It was election day. The noble Feud Leaders were extremely busy, keeping certain angry men apart, keeping them from discussing politics or drinking whiskey. I never saw more earnest effort.

Two small crowds of vengeful men were crossing the road in opposite directions, and about thirty feet apart as they crossed. A lad, about sixteen, in one of the crowds, suddenly drew a pistol and fired a shot into the ground. Instantly there was a flash of weapons, a deafening roar, and three men were lifeless on the ground while several more were wounded.

That lad had caught sight of the man who, years before, had slain his father. He fired the shot into the ground as a challenge to battle. He was seeking an opportunity to fire that other shot for which he had been in training all his life.

His opportunity came and he fired the shot with deadly precision. An old score was wiped out, but many new scores took its place. A feud was started which raged for three years and, in which, a hundred and fifty noble men lost their lives.

One Sunday morning my only living uncle took me out to the old family graveyard on the mountain side, where three generations of our people were buried.

A boy fires the fatal shot. The signal for deadly conflict and countless reprisals in life.

Untimely graves on the mountain side,
an irresistible call for volunteers.

There he pointed out many untimely graves, as he called them. Then sitting down on a mossy stone beneath a giant oak, he told me the strange stories of the pathetic tragedies.

His tones were earnest, reverential. There were tears in his voice as he portrayed in simple, graphic words the courage and valor of those who rested there. He made the battle scenes pass in living panorama in colors so vivid that I could almost hear the roar of the rifles and smell the burnt powder.

This was the call of the wild to me, for these were my own people—the people my father had left to fight alone.

I went straight into the battle line, determined to bear a double part—my own part and, also, the part which my father did not bear—determined to stop this merciless feud by exterminating the other fellows—determined to avenge the blood of my relatives who slept in those untimely graves.

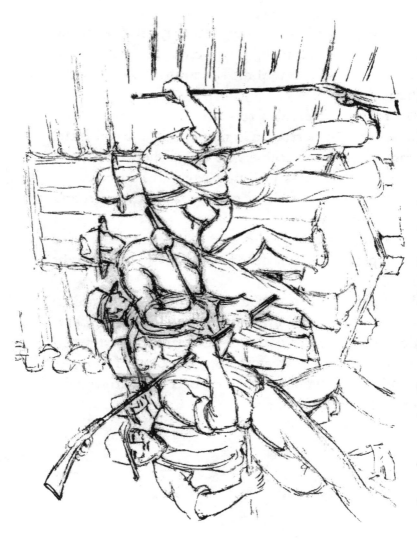

A complete surprise. They stole around the cabin and made a successful attack from the rear.

CHAPTER X.

The years that followed were crowded full of menace—days of danger, nights of waking. The battle was ever imminent, the clansmen ever ready.

I have seen the bravest of men and the noblest of boys, in perfect physical health, cut down instantly—one moment full of lusty life, the next, prone, helpless, inert.

The battles were never pitched. They were always purely incidental, brought on unexpectedly. Some reckless boy, or some irresponsible drunken man, would start the trouble. Then of course the others would join in.

My clothes were sometimes pierced by bullets. More than once I was left on the battle field for dead. But I passed through nearly four years of hair-breadth escapes without losing my own life or taking the life of another.

I regard the fact, that I did so, as a special providence. Nothing short of continual Divine protection and supervision could have brought a mortal through the exigencies of four such years without disastrous results of some kind.

One evening three of us charged a fortified cabin on

Weapons dismantled, but a thousand times more determined, that the feuds should be stopped.

Newfound. While we were trying to force the door the men who were on the inside climbed out at a little window, came around the cabin, fell in on our rear, lammed me over the head with a rifle, and threw me over the palings into a patch of tall weeds—dead. But I did not die.

When I regained consciousness the next morning I went to the top of a mountain, in the big woods, and spent three days and nights in lonely vigils. I did a lot of thinking. Was I still alive? How could it be possible?

The third night I slept and dreamed and awoke to the twilight songs of the wild birds. A change had come over my being. I was not the same—very different. The urge of vengeance was gone, and peace reigned within The whole world was new and beautiful.

According to my understanding, the blessed Holy Spirit (working in sovereign, solemn silence, as He always does without asking the consent of any mortal) had taken away the heart of stone and had given, in its place, a heart of flesh while I slept—a heart of mercy instead of a heart of vengeance.

I dismantled my guns. My feud days were over. But I was a thousand times more determined than ever that the feuds should be stopped—that their appalling toll of richest, reddest blood and superbest manhood should cease.

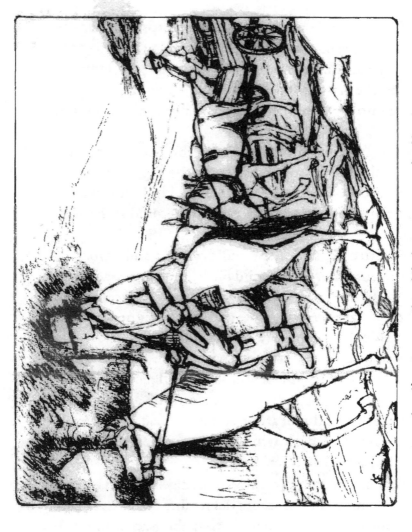

A perilous passage. Two of the bravest, truest and noblest men the Kentucky mountains ever produced; each was checkmated by the other.

CHAPTER XI.

During my four years of actual contact with the feuds and the feudists (I lived with them and on several occasions almost died with them) I made several important discoveries. My experiences and my observations forced me to various conclusions.

The mountaineers, taken as a whole, were just as brave and just as cowardly as any equal number of Anglo-Saxon people in any other section of our country. They had just as many brave men and just as many sneaking cowards, in proportion to population. A very few of them would actually sneak around and shoot from ambush.

Then men of mature age were not bloodthirsty beings, but the very reverse of it. They were the kindest, gentlest men I ever knew. They did not want the feuds. They would do anything in their power to stop the feuds. They sought, continually, to establish lasting covenants of peace.

This was especially true of the men who were spoken of as "Feud Leaders." Many people think that feud leaders are men who spend their lives laying schemes to get their enemies killed. Just the reverse is true. They are peace makers. They are simply the men to whom all eyes turn instinctively in time of trouble, for counsel and advice. There is no such office as "Feud Leader" known to our mountains. These men, so styled, are the men who happen to be of strongest personal influence and character. They used that strength of character and influence to bring about reconciliation and to avert bloodshed. Without them there would have been a continual reign of terror.

Here is an incident which shows, in clear light, the character of feud leaders. I shall call these two leaders "Mr. A" and "Mr. B." They are both special friends of mine. I have known them both, very intimately, for thirty years. They are both still living:

Mr. A and Mr. B had near relatives in a terrible fight on one election day. Several were killed and wounded. Every one felt certain that, when these two leaders met, there would be a battle to the death. Each one of these leaders believed, beyond doubt, that the other would shoot at sight.

A short time after the fight referred to above, Mr. A rode to church some five miles from his home. After services he started back. He soon overtook a man in a wagon, driving two mules. Looking down he discovered that the man in the wagon was Mr. B. Instantly Mr. A drew his pistol. He hesitated, then said to himself, "I can't shoot a man in the back. That would be murder. I can't turn and ride back the way I came. That would be cowardly. If I ride past him and he sees me he will kill me. What shall I do? I will ride past him, trust in God and fear not." So he spurred the horse and passed the wagon.

Mr. B looked up and saw that the passing horseman was Mr. A. Instantly Mr. B drew his pistol. He hesitated, then said to himself, "I can't shoot him. My life was in his hands. I was at his mercy and he didn't kill me."

Mr. A sold out his business and moved away. Mr. B laid down his guns and became a peaceable citizen. Both men told me, confidentially, about this perilous passage, and they told it just alike. They are still warm friends of mine, and Mr. B lives in Oneida.

These feud-battles were almost always precipitated by reckless boys, or by irresponsible, drunken men, in spite of the combined efforts and energies of the feud leaders and the men of experience. Through the influence of the leaders, covenants of peace were often established, all parties agreeing to leave adjustment to the courts. The fires of vengeance (never quite extinct) would smolder for a long time. Then, on some public occasion, a reckless boy would meet, face to face, with the slayer of his father. The boy would start a fight and then, inevitably, brave men would join in and fight to the death. The long-smoldering fires would blaze out afresh into fiercest flame, and the feud would rage again in devastating fury for years.

47

I knew there must be a solution for this problem, but, for the life of me, I could not figure it out. Still, I was certain that it could be found, and that our mountain children could be saved from the terrible curse. I would seek diligently till I found it. I would never abandon the quest.

How to keep the boys from starting feud-battles was "The Mountain Problem" — the problem which was breaking every mother's heart.

CHAPTER XII.

So I turned my back on the bloody scene, just as my father had done fifty years before. I went to my old home in West Virginia. There the Baptist Education Society discovered me and sent me to Dennison University. They would make a great scholar of me there, then send me to a Theological School and make a great preacher of me. They were thinking great things for me, in those days.

From my earliest recollection, I had seen visions of progress and achievement in the great world beyond the mountains. My heart yearned and pleaded dumbly for an opportunity to mix and mingle, to take my place in the march of cosmic progress and development. Now, at last, the opportunity had come. I went to Dennison.

I learned very little, of vital importance, from the books. But from the students, I learned how to solve the problem of the Cumberlands.

For four years I had been with the young feudists, in whose lives the spirit of vengeance reigned supreme, and in whose footsteps death and destruction followed.

But, in Dennison, I found four or five hundred splendid Christian young men and women, all working

Trying a new plan. The little fellows were starving for peace and sympathy. They welcomed the touch of a friendly hand.

in harmony, fellowship and peace. The contrast was sudden, startling. It set me thinking.

If our children of the mountains had faithful teachers, with hearts of love and the mind of the Master, would they not grow up to be splendid young people like these? Why not? In brain and brawn and blood they were the equals of any children on earth.

So I began praying to the Lord to send such teachers there. I kept this up for several weeks but there was no answer to my prayer. I grew restless—hesitant. I wondered.

Who was I that I should counsel the Lord and give Him directions? Did He not know? Had He not always known? Were not His attributes infinite — His wisdom, goodness, mercy, power?

Gradually, unobtrusively, as the morning twilight steals out of the darkness, a thought fixed itself in my mind, a determination gripped my soul. I would go myself instead of praying to Him to send others. I would make a beginning, myself. I would start something.

Perhaps this was the answer to my prayer. Perhaps this was why my father had left the feuds to live and die among strangers. Perhaps this was why the Education Society had sent me to Dennison — not, as they thought, to become a great scholar and a great preacher —but just to learn how to solve the problem of the feuds. Perhaps this was why I had spent four years with the feudists. Perhaps the Lord would send others to my assistance if only I had faith enough to throw myself into the breach. I would go. The labors of my life should be one continual, importunate appeal to Him, who works in us, both to *will* and to *do*.

I went at once, without telling even my school fellows what was hidden in my heart. Neither did I tell my relatives in the mountains. It was a secret between Him and me. Under sealed orders, I steered the virgin ship into the hazards of an uncharted sea.

I taught in the little log school houses winter and summer. I preached on Saturdays and Sundays. The burden of every lesson, every sermon, was *peace on earth and good will*.

Young people flocked to my schools. Boys would walk by my side and ask questions while they held to my hands. I scattered my work all over the country, seeking the most needy localities. I was in earnest.

The work was encouraging at first. The people, especially the children, readily accepted my teaching. It was easily seen that their simple hearts (just like the hearts of all other human beings) were hungry, starving for peace and happiness.

In a few months a community would be transformed. But when I left it and crossed the mountain into another valley, the old trouble would break out afresh. Some reckless boy would start a fight and then the feud would rage again.

This troubled me. Gradually I began to see that there must be a permanent school, serving as a centre and extending its circumference till the whole region was included.

The parting of the ways, at the cross roads of life.
Each man goes to his own calling.

CHAPTER XIII.

ABOUT this time my brother Bill came to visit with me. He stayed several weeks and looked the situation over carefully. When he was ready to start back to West Virginia he said: "Jim, you have thoroughly made up your mind to stay here?"

"Yes, thoroughly."

"Well, I want you to be perfectly frank and tell me what you see in this situation that leads you to this strange decision. I have wondered why you abandoned your opportunity at Dennison University, and why you insist on staying here. Many of your friends would like to know. Will you be perfectly frank and tell me why —keep nothing back?"

"Bill, I have always hesitated to speak of inner experiences—my own or other people's. It is too much like laying bare the heart for inspection. But, if you really want to know, I'll tell you."

"Well, I surely would like to know."

"In this situation, I can see that God has placed me here (called me and led me) to aid in saving five hundred thousand human beings from the terrible feud curse. I gave up my course at Dennison that I might answer this call."

"But in what way do you think He has called you and led you?"

"He has called me by giving me a heart which responds in deepest sympathy to this mute, importunate appeal for aid. By a vast conspiracy of circumstances He has led my steps to this very spot on which we stand. This is perfectly frank."

"Um——m! Fatalism!"

"It doesn't matter what you call these views, Bill. You may call them fatalism, Calvinism, or The Absolute Sovereignty of God. The term you use doesn't matter. You asked me to be perfectly frank with you, and I have done so."

"Daddy held the same views exactly."

"Yes, I have often heard you argue with him. At that time, I thought you were right. Now I think you were very——very wrong."

"Well, let me see, Jim——you are going to stay here because you have a sympathetic heart and an opportunity?"

"Yes."

"You think that God has given you both heart and opportunity for this very purpose?"

"Exactly."

"But can't you see that these things——all things—— are contingent?"

"In a sense, yes."

"Contingent, and yet predestinated? How can that be possible?"

"Why, Bill, it is only the paradox of life. It is ever recurrent. They crucified and slew our Savior, but God's hand and counsel had, long before, determined the same. Joseph's brethren sold him as a slave. They meant it for evil, but God meant it for good. It was God's way of sending Joseph before them to save their lives."

"But, Jim, these were *great* things in world history —*special providences*. Our *trivial* affairs are not to be compared with such things as these."

"Who shall decide which things are great and which are small in God's sight, Bill? Consider the lilies of the field, the ravens, the sparrows, the falling hairs. God cares for all these. To my mind all things are predestinated or nothing is—if one thing is, then all must be —if not all, then not one."

"Jim, this is mighty hard to believe."

"Yes, I know it is mighty hard to believe, but the other thing is much *harder* to believe."

"What other thing?"

"Why, that Almighty God is not Almighty—that He cannot, or *will* not, do His will in the army of Heaven and among the inhabitants of the earth."

"You argue in a circle, Jim, just as Daddy did. This makes argument futile and interminable."

"All argument is so. But, Bill, I am not arguing. You

asked me to be frank. Blame me or not, just as you like. I have only laid bare my heart."

"But how do you propose to stop the feuds?"

"I don't propose to stop them."

"What then?"

"I propose to teach the children of the hostile clans to love each other. This done, the feuds will stop automatically."

"How can you do this?"

"Gather them into a school at the earliest possible age. Make peace and good will the foundation of every lesson. Overcome, in this way, the hatred and vengeance which they learn in their homes."

"Are they taught vengeance in their homes?"

"Intentionally, no. Incidentally, yes."

"What do you mean, incidentally?"

"Do you remember the bloody, bullet-riddled shirt which the woman showed you last Sunday?"

"Yes, I do."

"You remember the little boy who stood by her knee and listened in stolid silence?"

"Yes, I remember him very well."

"Well, Bill, that boy will certainly avenge that blood and those tears if love doesn't take the place of vengeance in his heart."

"But they have lots of preachers. Why don't they hear the Gospel?"

"They hear the Gospel only once each month. They hear the story of the bloody shirt every day. It is the one subject of vital interest in their homes."

"Well, it seems to me that you are putting education before the Gospel."

"No, Bill, I certainly do not. The *fact* of the Gospel is one thing—the *proclamation* of the Gospel is quite another thing. The fact of the Gospel may be preached, proclaimed, by a friend, a mother, a teacher. Anyone who tells the story of the Cross is a real preacher. He may not be the pastor of a church, he may not be even ordained to preach. But if he tells the sinner of a loving Savior he certainly is preaching, proclaiming the Gospel in the most vital sense. In the school which lives in my visions and dreams, the fact of the Gospel (Christ crucified) preludes, permeates, and postludes every lesson. The teacher's desk, the play ground, the work shop, each of these shall be a pulpit."

"Do you mean that you will try to build such a school?"

"God helping me I will try to build it."

"I am sorry, Jim. Better go back to West Virginia with me. It is a broader field of usefulness. You will find lots of churches there ready to support you well if you preach for them. You will starve if you stay here. Better pull up-stakes, Jim, and go with me."

"No, Bill, I have seen plenty of these broader fields

of usefulness; but when you survey them you find that they are not broader at all. It is the larger salary which makes them look broader. I don't want to preach *for* people but *to* them. I want to preach *for* the Lord *to* the people. To my mind, there is a world of difference between preaching *to* people and *for* people."

"What do you mean, Jim?"

"Why, Bill, if I preach *for* a church they will tell me what they want me to preach, and if I do it they will support me. If I fail to preach what they want me to preach they will turn me off. If I preach *for* the Lord He certainly will support me in His own way. I am not afraid to trust Him."

"Well, I am sorry, but I must go, Jim."

"Bill, don't go. Stay here with me and help me. These are as much your people as mine. You can do a great work here."

"No, Jim, I go to my own work. Good-bye."

He rode away, and I was left alone.

CHAPTER XIV.

A short time after this I met Rev. H. L. McMurry, a Baptist preacher from Kansas. He encouraged me greatly. His vision for the mountains was the same as mine, his faith in God the same.

Together we went to Oneida, my father's boyhood home, and the centre of the "Baker-Howard Feud" which was raging there at that time. Together we planned the beginnings of Oneida Institute.

After several weeks spent in riding over the mountains we secured a meeting of the mountaineers, in an old mill shed—the site of many bloody battles—right where our school buildings are now standing.

There were half a hundred of these men. They represented both sides of the feud. They were the best and the bravest men we knew. Many of them had ugly scars on their bodies. All of them had bitter memories in their hearts—memories of untimely graves on the mountain sides.

They sat there facing each other in silence. A tenseness filled the atmosphere. It was a dangerous thing to bring them together there. One single wrong move would have precipitated a terrible battle.

As I looked into their faces—faces I knew so well—

61

Let's build a school and teach our children to love each other.
If we do this the feuds will stop automatically.

I realized that the opportunity of my life had come at last—the one thing for which I had been born and for which my life had been spared.

Nothing doubting, I stepped to the middle of the old shed between the hostile clans. I said:

"Men, I know as well as you do that you do not want this feud—that you are trying to stop it. But I know, also, that your methods are wrong. We cannot stop this feud by killing each other. Every drop of blood we shed will call for hundreds more and will entail a curse on our children to the seventh generation. We have been teaching our children to hate each other for a hundred years, and we have had destruction and death as a result. Let's try another plan. Let's teach our children to love each other and then we will have peace."

I said, "Men, let's all join in together and build us a little school of our own, put our children into it at the earliest possible age, and teach them the story of our Savior's love every hour in the day. When they learn that story of dying love, and contrast it with the cruel, murderous love of the feudists, they will never seek each other's lives again. But peace will come into our hearts and into our little cabin homes."

There were several other points I had planned that I would urge on that crowd of feudists, but I was interrupted. Lee Combs, a man who had been at war with our family since his boyhood, sprang up and came walking rapidly toward me. Then I noticed that Frank Burns, a cousin of mine, was walking just as rapidly from the other side. It seemed that both men were trying to reach me first, like tackles or guards in a football game. Then I saw that all the men were deliberately walking to the centre of the old shed, while they looked into each other's faces with level eyes. A tenseness throbbed through the atmosphere. What would the result be?

But Combs halted, turned around, raised his hand high above his head and said, "Boys, let's do that if it's the last act of our lives."

My eyes overflowed with tears of gratitude. Instantly all those men were mixing and mingling with each other, each one grasping the hand of every other one in solemn covenant. I realized that God had given me more than I had dared to hope—that the feuds were ended.

CHAPTER XV.

ONE sultry afternoon of the following week, Mc-Murry and I climbed up into the branches of a large oak tree which grew on a hill overlooking the beautiful valley. The view was magnificent—the confluence of the three little rivers—Bull Skin, Goose Creek and Red Bird—forming the south fork of the Kentucky; the little valley—an emerald nestling there—like Jerusalem, surrounded by the everlasting hills; and, yes, there was Mount Moriah, a little hill in the middle of the valley. We would build on that.

There were only three residences in Oneida at that time—two cottages and one hewed-log house. Besides these, there were a country store in which the postoffice was kept, and a round-log stable on the top of Mount Moriah. Bob Carnahan operated the store and the post-office. The whole valley was a rye field that year.

With this vision of beauty before us, we drafted the charter of Oneida Institute and wrote the names of a score of men who, we thought, would make good Trustees. Then we discussed ways and means of operation.

McMurry said, "Burns, this school will grow into a great institution, because it is purely the work of God which cannot be overthrown. He has directed our footsteps right into the branches of this tree."

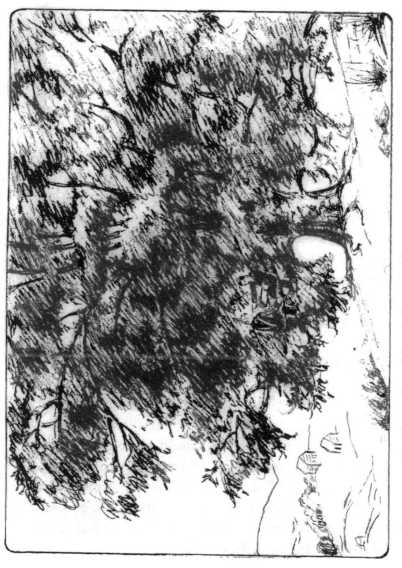

The Charter Oak of Oneida Institute where visions and dreams began to take the form of realities. The birthplace of a school.

I said, "Yes, McMurry, I do believe that He has led us all the way, and that nothing can thwart His purpose in our lives."

He was silent a long time, then said, "When we have organized our Board of Trustees, they will elect you President." I replied, "No, no, McMurry, I couldn't think of such a thing as that. I could never do it. I have no education to speak of—just what I have dug up by myself. Then I am entirely unknown. You are a school man, a man of large acquaintance. You are the one man qualified to head our school."

"It can never be," he replied. "You may not be a man of the schools, but you are a man of the mountains. These people know you and trust you. You are one of them. They will follow you. No other man on earth could lead them. You will always be the real President of this school and the real pastor of this church, even though someone else should hold the official position. I feel that God sent me here to find you, help you start the school and introduce you and your work to such friends as He has given me. When that is done, I shall go to some other field, but my heart will always be in the Highlands."

I was silent but rebellious. From earliest childhood, I had shrunk from publicity of any kind. Still, deep down in my heart, I realized that a prophet had spoken. But I was determined to shift the responsibility if possible. The same feeling abides with me still. I don't mind fighting in the ranks as a private, but to be a General, a leader, is a cross almost too heavy. "If I do this willingly, I have a reward; but, if against my will, a dispensation is committed unto me." Moses, Gideon, Jonah and many others rebelled.

We climbed down from the charter oak our souls more firmly knit together by the similarity of our visions and our dreams. No matter where he labors nothing can separate me from the soul of McMurry. Others may take their own places in my life. None can ever take the place of McMurry—his own place.

The next Saturday we met in an old log church house and organized our first Board of Trustees, selecting twelve of the best men we had. But when we were ready to sign the charter of Oneida Institute it was found that more than half our trustees couldn't even write their names—had to make their marks. And yet, they were going to build an educational institution.

The first item of business they transacted was my selection as President of that school, and there wasn't even a particle of that school there to be president of.

So there I was, forty miles from the nearest railroad, without a dollar, no source of income whatever, and with less than two years' schooling to serve as my qualification for the presidency of that impossibility. It was the testing time of faith.

68

But I did not hesitate. I took two old crowbars, carried them on my shoulder to Mart Doyle's blacksmith shop, cut them into pieces, and out of the pieces, made a crude set of stone cutter's tools. Then I went to work and laid the foundation of our first school building with my own hands.

"This is the loft out of my house."
What a gift! It was zero weather, too.

Laying the Corner stone of Oneida Institute.
An imposing ceremony, not reported until now.

CHAPTER XVI.

THE most momentous event of my life, in a peculiar sense, was the laying of the corner stone. For two weeks I had been thinking about it while working—clearing the site and dressing the stones with my crude tools. Should I notify McMurry and the trustees, arrange a program, and proceed in the regular way? Or should I go on with the work without emphasizing, in any way, the placing of this first stone?

At last my mind was made up. I would lay the stone, but it should be a private personal matter between the Master Builder and me. He would know, but no one else should. I would not tell even McMurry.

The occasion should be secret, sacred, solemn—like the prayer in the closet with the door shut. Had I not been working, silently, to this end for seven long, weary years? I would hide it in my heart, along with some other treasures too sacred to be exploited.

With this conclusion firmly fixed, I made all the necessary preparations the day before. Then, in the early morning twilight, with a friendly, cloudless sky bending above me, I walked slowly to the little campus and quietly placed the prepared stone in its prepared place.

Then I bowed my head in something like a prayer—just a few spontaneous, unspoken words, the silent appeal of a heart too full for utterance. Even a whisper would have been out of place.

But, somehow I felt that I was not all alone, that a Presence was with me. Then I thought of the three Hebrew boys who walked through the flames, not by themselves, but accompanied by another whose form was like the Son of God.

As I turned away to go to breakfast the sun's first rays were kissing into golden splendor the peaks of the Bull Skin mountains, the mists were rolling in beautiful billows of silver from the valleys, the atmosphere was instinct with the subtle fragrance of budding hope, and the mocking birds were singing in the big elm tree nearby.

Suddenly the staccato sounds of a volley of shots pierced the peaceful atmosphere. A young feudist was riding recklessly up the river bank and firing his pistol into the air.

But the corner stone was laid. The ceremony was over. The Rubicon was crossed. I had pledged my life. The gift was on the altar, and all the results in the hands of the Eternal. I would never again question His ability to clothe and feed. I would work on and on—walk blind to the darkness before from the darkness behind.

After this I went about the work with a strange feeling of peace in my heart—a peace which the continual crises attending more than a quarter of a century of incessant toil have never, in the least, disturbed. I have never, for one little minute, doubted that He who clothes the lilies will much more clothe the laborers whom He sends into His vineyard.

But I didn't work many more days by myself. The mountaineers came to the rescue, just as I knew they would. Some pledged lumber, some labor. Big Henry

Hard pillows, but wonderfully peaceful.
These men were building a schoolhouse which
no one had hired them to build.

73

Hensley gave me fifty dollars, the first money I received. Bob Carnahan gave me twenty-five dollars. All these—the money, the fellow workers, the encouragement—I regarded as gifts straight from Above.

In a very short time, twenty sturdy mountaineers were working side by side. It seemed strange, almost unthinkable, to see these men who represented different sides of the feuds, working there together unarmed. Some of them had ugly scars on their bodies. All of them had painful wounds in their hearts. But I held out to them the hope of peace, and they were actually working there in perfect harmony and without the least fear of each other. I believe that they would have plucked out their eyes and given them to me.

We often worked till midnight and then slept on the shavings under the work benches. We were building a school house, not because someone had hired us to build it, but because we loved our mountain children and wanted to free them from the terrible feud curse.

The motive of service makes all the difference in the world in the day's work. If we work because we love, every day will be too short, and the most painful task will be a pleasure. The hireling sees the danger approaching and flees. The Good Shepherd thrusts himself between the flock and the danger and lays down his life for the sheep. This is just as true today as it was on the shores of Galilee two thousand years ago.

Big Henry Hensley.

And so the work progressed. We planned to open school January first, nineteen hundred.

It was now Christmas, the snow was deep and the ice frozen thick on the river. We lacked four hundred feet of lumber and four days' work of having our building ready.

But our mill was broken, we had no lumber, and the case seemed hopeless.

I went to the unfinished school house early in the morning. The workmen were standing idly around in gloomy silence. They looked at me hopelessly, their souls in their eyes. I, too, was silent.

Soon, an ox team, drawing a loaded wagon, was seen crossing the river on the ice. It approached, turned off of the road and onto the campus, drove up to the building and began unloading planks—dry, smoke-stained, yellow poplar planks.

I said, "Where did you get it, Frank?" He replied, "It is the loft out of my house." He had taken the loft out of his little cabin home and hauled it to the school house in zero weather. What a gift!

The workmen seized planks, before the wagon was unloaded, and hastened to the work benches. For two days and nights the planes sang, the hammers rang, and the work was completed. The house was ready.

CHAPTER XVII.

THE next Monday morning fires were built in the stoves, the bell was rung and the doors were thrown open. One hundred boys and girls, young men and young women, crowded in to apply for places as students. Then came the citizens and pressed into the little chapel till there was no longer standing room. Dr. M. P. Hunt, of Louisville, Ky., whose services McMurry had enlisted, made the opening address. He spoke out of his great sympathetic heart a real message of encouragement. His words stirred our souls.

I arose and faced the audience. As I looked into the earnest faces of my people I read there a pledge of perpetual loyalty. As I looked into the hopeful faces of one hundred students I read there the infallible prophecy of a coming brighter better day—a little cloud, like the hand of a man on the dim, distant horizon. I realized that my life work had at last begun.

That was twenty-six years ago—a long, long time—and yet it seems but a day. I have been too busy to note the lapse of time.

The problem was before us, a faculty of three. I was particularly fortunate in having the assistance of H. L. McMurry and C. A. Dugger as teachers.

We had classes ranging from the primary to the

77

All ages, sexes and sizes. Full grown men recited in the classes with little children.

Eighth grade. Full grown men recited in the same classes with little children.

We charged one dollar a month for tuition, but very few of our students were able to pay it. The tuition fund would scarcely pay the coal bills. One boy brought a sheep skin and said, "Maybe this will pay my tuition for this month." We cut the sheep skin into pieces and used it for erasers.

But, through the influence of McMurry, we had made a few faithful friends. Occasionally a small check would come. We divided it among ourselves, equally, and worked on.

Our student body increased to two hundred The responsibility was tremendous. We had before us, in every class, little children who really hated each other —had been taught to hate each other in their cradles. Our task was to lead them to love each other, and, while doing so, to teach them as much grammar and arithmetic as we could.

To this end we had chapel services each morning, and a hymn service each noon. We kept the love of our Savior and the Golden Rule before our students every hour in the day.

In a very short time a few of our older students caught the vision and began to help us. They made the work much lighter for us, and their moral support was a great encouragement. Several faithful workers were soon added to our faculty—Louis Sandlin, Dan Hacker, Luther Hatton, and Luther Johnston. They were all native mountaineers. What an inspiration it was to work with such men! Their hearts were as the heart of one man. For long years we labored, our elbows touching. We didn't talk with each other very much. We just worked. It was a real case of coöperation. How we loved each other and our students! And how our students loved us!

At the end of the first year, McMurry was forced to leave us on account of the needs of his growing family. The next year, Dugger followed him, and the work was left to the native mountaineers.

There was not a scholar in our faculty. Our advanced class had learned all that we could teach them. They knew as many things as we knew, except *one;* we knew that they did, and they didn't know it. We were the best scholars by such odds, only.

They clamored for a High School course. We held a faculty meeting and decided to learn the lessons over night which we were going to teach them the next day.

For many long months we kept this up—sometimes with smoky lanterns in a classroom till the midnight hour, sometimes by a driftwood fire on the river bank while we fished for a meat supply for next day, and thought of the fishermen who, long ago, sought for tribute money in the mouth of a fish.

The signing of a covenant which had lived in the hearts of these men for many months.

Did putting it on the blackboard make it any more binding?

One night, when our lessons for the next day were learned, we sat in silence for a few minutes. Then I went to the blackboard and wrote this sentence and signed my name below it: "We agree to work on till the end of each month, take what money the Lord has sent us, pay off the grocery bills for our helpless students, and then divide equally among ourselves whatever is left over."

I went back to my seat. Not a word was spoken. Dan Hacker went to the board and wrote his name below mine, then Louis Sandlin, then Luther Hatton, then Luther Johnston. Still, not a word was spoken. We each went home in silence.

There is one incident connected with the signing of this covenant which I have not told. Those who signed will remember it well, and, also, one other person will remember it. For my part it is a sealed book.

For several years the average pay of a teacher was fourteen dollars a month. But, somehow, we managed to live, and very well, too. We worked with our hands at various things. We caught fish. We rented land and raised gardens and crops in summer.

One morning I ate breakfast with Dan Hacker. As we finished, Lucinda said, "This is our last piece of meat." Dan and I walked into the yard. He said, "What will we do today?" I replied, "Let's finish laying by our corn crop."

Without another word we crossed Goose Creek in a little boat, got our hoes, and went to work. At eleven o'clock the last row had been hoed, and we started home. The crop was laid by.

When we reached the river it was very muddy, and swollen about a foot. There had been a heavy rain the night before on the head waters. I paddled the boat. It struck something which was not there when we crossed in the morning. I stopped paddling. Dan reached into the muddy water and drew up a fish basket, a sort of trap. It had fourteen very large catfish in it—meat for several days. It had floated down the river from somewhere. We never knew.

We didn't talk about it, but I saw a strange light in Dan's eyes. Coincidence? Yes, undoubtedly. But who controls and directs all the coincidences of life, even the very small and, seemingly, insignificant ones? Believe as you may, but let me believe as I may. It encourages my heart in troublous times to think that our Heavenly Father knows and tempers every wind that blows.

All in all, we were having a pretty tough time, though extremely interesting. There was nothing the least bit insipid about it. The greatest hardship, perhaps, was learning the lessons over night. But at these nightly seances we always prayed for the Lord to send us a real scholar, someone who would not have to pioneer in Latin and Geometry.

A fish basket with fourteen large catfish in it had floated down the river from somewhere and had stopped in the right place at the right time.

One summer day, at noon, I sat on the porch of my little cabin home. A young man, tall, dignified, prepossessing, rode up to the gate, dismounted, came in and said, "I am John Henry Walker. You influenced my father to send me to Georgetown College. I have come to work with you if you need me."

We needed him—a man of sterling qualities, a son of the mountains, one of the most efficient teachers I have ever known. He became the pride and the prodigy of our school. He bore the burden that had been crushing the life out of us. We almost worshipped him.

There was no more learning of midnight lessons. One whole year he gave his services without one penny of remuneration. At last he was forced to give up his work with us and go to a farm. But I surely believe that the Lord will make it possible for him to come back and finish his days in the work he loves. He married one of our school girls, a girl who never can forget her mountain home. The Lord will surely send him back, sometime, somehow.

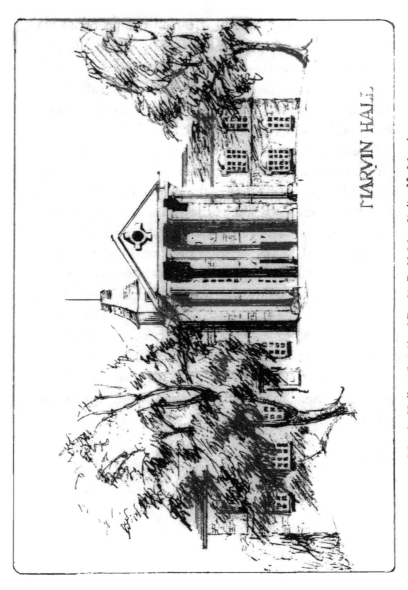

MARVIN HALL

Marvin Hall—The gift of Dr. J. B. & Mrs. Juliet N. Marvin.

CHAPTER XVIII.

WHEN our school began its work there were only two residences in Oneida—two little cabin homes. The people who lived in these cabins kept all the students possible, and the rest stayed in homes, one to three miles away. They walked through the mud and waded the swollen streams.

But before the first year's work was ended a half dozen new homes had been built. Men who were interested in the education of their children bought lots and built homes. This was a great help. Our students could get places to live close to the school. This is the way Oneida, a town of one hundred homes, has been built up. It makes an ideal village.

In the spring of nineteen hundred McMurry got a letter from a friend of his, Dr. Carter Helm Jones, of Louisville, Ky., saying that if he and I would come to the meeting of the State Board of Missions he (Jones) thought he could get some support for our work. McMurry said, "We will go and take a chance." The day came, the day on which we must start. I hadn't a penny, neither had McMurry. But we planned to ride to East Burnstead, our nearest railroad point. If Mr. Brownlee, the agent, couldn't get us a pass we would ride back home.

Dr. J. B. Marvin.

Mrs. J. B. Marvin.
(Juliet N. Marvin.)

Accordingly, we saddled our mules and hitched them at the gate while we ate dinner. The mail arrived from Burning Springs, and brought us a check for fifty dollars. We went, rejoicing, but we didn't talk about it.

Broadway Baptist Church, of Louisville, gave us seventy dollars a month, indefinitely. What a blessing! It made it possible for us to live.

In June, 1901, I got a wire from the same Carter Helm Jones. It said, "Come to Louisville at once." When I arrived, he took me to the home of Dr. J. B. Marvin. We talked over all the situation thoroughly. No one decided anything definitely. I went back home, wondering what the result would be.

In a very few days I got another wire, saying, "Dr. and Mrs. Marvin have decided to give five thousand dollars for a building." This was more money than I had ever thought of before. I was astonished. Mrs. Marvin also pledged thirty dollars a month for the support of a teacher. This made one hundred dollars a month for expenses. It was almost too good to believe.

J. H. Blackburn, a contractor and builder of Barbourville, Ky., took the contract for the new building. We burned the bricks, sawed the lumber, dressed it and did all the work with our own hands. The building had a chapel and six large recitation rooms—the first brick building in, or near, Oneida. Mrs. Marvin's name is still a watchword in our mountain homes.

*The three girls who failed to get into the school, but who inspired
the building of Carnahan Hall.*

In the winter of 1905, an old gentleman came to my home late in the evening. He brought with him his daughter and two of his nieces. The four of them had ridden forty miles on two mules.

While we were eating supper, one of the girls said, "Mr. Burns, we have come to school. We heard that there was a school here in which girls could work out their education." I didn't reply.

The next morning, after breakfast, I told them that we had turned away more than one hundred, already, for lack of room and work—that there was no possible place for them.

I watched them as they mounted the two mules and rode away. I saw that their cheeks were wet with tears of disappointment, as, with breaking hearts, they started back to the hopelessness of their fated lives. When they had disappeared, I uttered a prayer, I made a pledge, involuntarily: I would build a dormitory for girls if only the good Lord would let me live till the close of that semester.

When commencement was over, that spring, I wrote to Mr. Blackburn, the man who had built Marvin Hall. He came to Oneida. I told him that I wanted a dormitory for fifty girls at a cost of ten thousand dollars; that I hadn't a penny; but that I would go out on the face of the earth and raise the money while he was building the house.

CARNAHAN HALL

Carnahan Hall.

Robert Carnahan.

Mrs. Robert Carnahan.

He drew a plan and specifications, and said it could be done for ten thousand dollars. We consulted Bob Carnahan. He said, "Go on and build the house." Mr. Blackburn drew up the contract and we signed it.

The next week he brought workmen from Barbourville and began laying the foundation. I started out into the big, busy world. When I reached Carrolton, at the mouth of the Kentucky River, paid for my breakfast, and walked up to the meeting place of a District Association, I had twenty cents and a contract for a ten thousand dollar building in my pocket—that was all I had.

But I kept on going from place to place, wherever there was an open door. Somehow the pay rolls were always met. Bob Carnahan was holding the ropes, and paying all overdrafts. The result was that "Carnahan Hall" was completed in due time and a school home for fifty girls was provided. In some kind of a mystic sense, it was the gift of the old gentleman and the three heartbroken girls. I don't know what became of them. I never heard of them again. But the house still stands.

CHAPTER XIX.

THE school became more crowded each year. We turned away more students than we enrolled—lack of room and work. We couldn't furnish productive labor for so many of those eager, earnest mountain boys and girls who clamored for a fighting chance—a chance to work their way up and out.

So we labored on under appalling difficulties, our friends and their benefactions increasing barely enough to keep our teachers from getting too cold or too hungry. Difficulties, seemingly insuperable, came thick and fast. We never knew the source from which the next day's rations would come. We had no assurance whatever. The Board of Trustees took no financial responsibility. They simply met from time to time, discussed our problems, advised us, blessed us, and left the work entirely in our hands.

We didn't know what we could do, but we knew what we could not do—we could not abandon our work. Therefore, we left the results in God's hands. We had faith in Him. We, also, had confidence in people made in His image. We believed that, if the good people of this world could only know our problem, they would help us solve it. If they could only understand our needs, our helplessness, and the magnificent possibili-

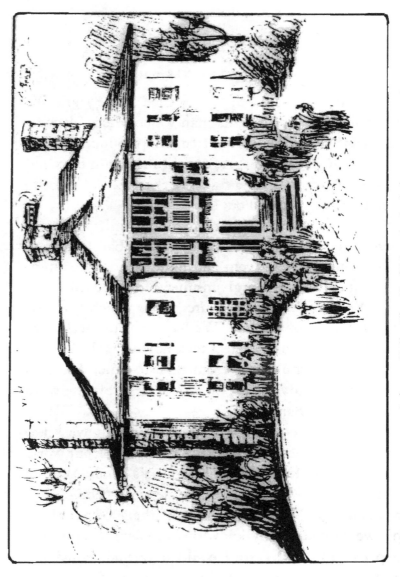

Anderson Hall—The gift of Mrs. A. A. Anderson.

ties hidden away in the blighted lives of our mountain children, they would come to the rescue.

But how could we get them to understand? Surrounded by affluence and opportunity, as they were, how could they understand the merciless difficulties which barred the way of life for us?

At last it was suggested that I go to New York and try to secure aid there. I objected strenuously. I rebelled. Being of retiring nature, almost diffident, I naturally shrank from publicity of any kind. But New York! It was entirely beyond me. My very soul protested. I was not equal to such a gigantic task.

For many days and nights the battle raged. I thought of the incongruities attending my appearance before a New York audience—a native Kentucky mountaineer, uncouth, uncultured. Then I thought of our children of the mountains—their yearning hearts, their pathetic struggle to break away from the cruel bondage of illiteracy.

But maybe God would use my message to the New Yorkers as a means of securing aid for our boys and girls who were struggling upward, ever upward to a higher plane of life. Would I go for them, and risk it? Would I trust the results to the Almighty? Yes, I would. I would go for them, and trust in God.

Just as I had reached this decision, Thomas L. Walker, of Lexington, Ky., one of the best and bravest friends I ever had, volunteered to go with me and stay a month. I rejoiced. He was a city-bred man, and I could lean on him.

Accordingly, in November, 1908, Tom and I walked out of Grand Central Station onto Forty-second Street. The night was dark, cold, foggy. Tom asked an officer the way to the old Astor House. He pointed to a hole in the sidewalk and said, "City Hall."

We descended into the subway and thundered down to the Astor House, where we stayed two nights.

But the prices were too high—one dollar and fifty cents each per day. We went room hunting, and thought ourselves lucky to find a room over a restaurant, on Forty-second Street, for six dollars a week, each.

Here we made our headquarters, and tried to keep our eating expenses down to one dollar a day. We were just a little bit hungry sometimes.

Through the kindness of Dr. Alderman of Louisville, Ky., I had been given an opportunity of addressing the Ministers' Conference.

Well, Monday morning came and Tom and I went to the Conference. It was a big room, and it was full of preachers—three or four hundred of them. But there was not one familiar face in the vast crowd.

They transacted their business with a snap and decision which, to me, was incredible. There was no circumlocution whatever. They struck to the point.

But I discovered, at once, that they were men—that they had hearts and heads—that some of them did violence to the Queen's English—that they were sometimes wrong in their conclusions, because they disagreed with each other.

The business transacted, the president said, "Mr., Burns will now address us for twenty-five minutes on Feud Conditions in the Cumberlands. He comes to us highly recommended."

I took the floor and faced the audience. I forgot my trepidation. I forgot everything but the helpless children at home and the struggling little school at the mouth of Red Bird. I was talking to the friends of my Master.

Interest was intense. Sympathy and understanding beamed in every eye. I could see that I was telling them nothing new—to them, it was just the old, old story of Jesus and His love. What a simpleton I had been to be afraid of my brethren—the friends of my Master!

When I had finished, they passed a resolution opening their hearts and their churches to me. This started a series of addresses extending all over New York and Brooklyn, and continuing for three months. I spoke at prayer meetings, banquets, missionary meetings, and such like. They were always cordial, but they took no definite steps, financially. New York acts with great deliberation.

Of course, this had a depressing effect on Tom and me. Deliberations were all right, and necessary, if someone didn't starve while the deliberations were in progress.

We didn't say anything about it to each other—we talked less and less, became almost silent in our little room. This lack of definite action was taking the life out of us both, and we were becoming more silent every day. How we suffered in silence! It bound us mighty close together, so close that words were unnecessary. We were firmer friends in desperation. We had done what we could, but New York did not move. Large bodies move slowly.

When we had been there about three weeks, I had an engagement to address the Ladies' Home Mission Society of Madison Avenue Baptist Church. It was the windiest, rainiest day I ever saw. I started. Tom was sick—didn't go. The church was eight blocks away. Before I had walked two blocks the wind wrecked my umbrella. When I arrived I was wet to the skin and cold.

There were about one dozen women present. The president introduced me, very formally, and I spoke for thirty minutes. I don't know what I said but I do know that I was never further away from hope and sunshine in all my life. I was in the depths, in every sense of the word.

When the address was finished I started to the door. One lady invited me to take luncheon with them. I excused myself and went on. Another lady followed me to the elevator and said, "Mr. Burns, just what is it you want?" I replied, "I want a farm for our boys." "How much will it cost?" she asked. I said, "Fifty-three hundred dollars." She said, "Take this card and call me up at nine-thirty in the morning. Our exchange is a private one."

When I looked at the card I almost fainted. The name was one of the most illustrious in New York—a name to conjure with in financial circles.

I called her on the phone as she requested. She said, "Come up to the house at four this afternoon." I went right into that marble palace and talked with her for an hour or more. She was charming, very cordial, but noncommittal.

The next day I got a letter from her with a check for fifty-three hundred dollars. She said, "Here is your farm." I lost sight of her during the World War and have not heard from her since. But the farm is still in operation.

I stayed two months after Tom left me and was busy every day. Out of that visit has grown Anderson Hall, costing eleven thousand dollars, one thousand acres of coal and timber land, and a host of friends who still contribute to the support of Oneida Institute.

Oneida as it appeared in 1899.

CHAPTER XX.

ONEIDA INSTITUTE has grown out of an indomitable purpose to stop the feuds and, in doing so, to conserve the manhood and the womanhood of the mountaineers. It never was a mission station in the common acceptation of the term. It has been purely indigenous from the very first—an uprising of the mountaineers themselves. In this, it is, perhaps, a little bit different from any other school.

It was, first, a vision; then, a hope; then, a prayer; then, a determination to—build. From every rational viewpoint, it was absolutely impossible. In a certain sense, it might well be considered as an act of desperation. To some of us, it was far better to work and faint and fall and fail rather than live and die on the battlefield of the feuds.

But, though the whole enterprise has been full of purpose and determination, there has been very little planning. We have been facing emergencies every day and every hour. Even now, as I am writing this, there are a dozen crying needs, all of which seem to be imperative. Our means are barely sufficient to meet one of the twelve. We are facing the perplexing problem of relative importance. Which shall it be?

When we were building our first school house, and

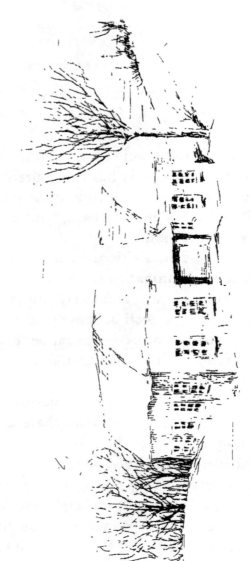

First Building Erected in 1899.

sleeping on beds of shavings, we never stopped to think of the possibility of having to build another house. That one building required all our means and all our strength. We hoped that it would be sufficient to serve our purpose and to solve our problem.

But, on the very first day of school, we discovered that our house was not half large enough. The one hundred students which we turned away were just as needy, just as worthy, and just as importunate as the ones we enrolled. It was the old problem of supply and demand. The demand upon our school has always been great, our supply always meager—quite inadequate. This forced us to lengthen the cords and strengthen the stakes in the face of difficulties which seemed insuperable.

After fourteen years of continuous crises, it became apparent, to those on the inside, that Oneida Institute was destined to be a school much larger than all our visions and dreams. It was also apparent that, if its supplies should be made equal to the demands upon it, we must manage in some way to secure the aid of a multitude of real friends. The various Boards, Societies, and Foundations seemed to be already overrun with demands from the regular channels. In order to secure the necessary number of friends, it would be necessary for us to go far afield, and to do a vast amount of broadcasting. But how could it be done? I prayed earnestly and long for the opportunity.

It came, but in a way of which I had never dreamed. The lecture bureaus offered me the very opportunity for which I had prayed.

This offer had every appearance of being purely accidental and contingent. God's providence always seems to be accidental when we look from the human viewpoint.

The presidents of the lecture bureaus are numbered among the greatest and noblest men on earth. But I don't suppose they ever suspected that, in offering this opportunity, they were answering a prayer. It is in this way that all things work together for good. The Lord directs the contingencies which determine the actions of men.

I gladly, and gratefully, accepted the offer, and followed the long, long trail which wound its way all over every state in the Union for twelve weary years. I delivered four thousand lectures to two million people. Every lecture was my best possible effort to secure friends for Oneida Institute and our mountain children.

If five percent of the people, in my audiences, were vitally interested, then Oneida Institute has one hundred thousand faithful friends scattered over all the various states. The friendship of these, when materilized, should result in sufficient facilities to meet emergencies and supply the demands made upon our school.

CHAPTER XXI.

In the Fall of 1921, it was discovered that our finances were in bad shape. The continuous pressing demands of the World War, the reaction which followed, together with an unfortunate administration, had almost completely wrecked our School.

An investigation showed that we owed nearly thirty-two thousand dollars. Our credit was no good. Banks would not make loans. Grocery houses would not sell us food. Dr. Adams resigned. Several of our teachers left us. To all outward appearances, our case seemed hopeless. Our property would be sold to pay the debts.

The Trustees held a meeting and agreed to make an effort to find a man to take the place of Dr. Adams. Louis Sandlin took charge of the School till such a man could be found. A few of our teachers, whose faithful hearts were always true, volunteered to keep up the classroom work. The citizens, out of their penury, made up a fund to support the teachers. I went about my lectures for the Bureaus, just as I had been doing since 1914. But my heart was very painfully sad.

The Trustees made several attempts to find their man. But no man, big enough and brave enough, could be found.

I was informed of all the numerous failures. But I

Mrs. Sylvia W. Russell.
Acting President of Oneida Institute.

refused even to think about it. That was the one thing I didn't dare to do. Thinking meant conclusion. Conclusion meant heart-breaking failure. Rational thought was a poor friend in those days. Refusing to think, I just worked on and trusted the results in the hands of Him.

At last, the Trustees held a meeting at Lexington, and failed to find their man.

H. G. Garrett (than whom a greater man has never lived) returned to his home, in Winchester, completely discouraged.

He said to his wife, "I believe that Oneida is lost. We can't get a man to take the place of Dr. Adams. The debts are too large and the conditions too discouraging. They are all afraid except Burns and his fool teachers. It's like trying to sell a dead horse."

His daughter, Daily, overheard the remark and said, "Daddy, why don't you try Mrs. Russell? I learned many things in her School at St. Helens. One of the many things I learned is that she is fearless, and that she can do anything which can be done. Try her. She can save Oneida if it is possible."

Mr. Garrett replied, "All right. We will try. It is a wonder I hadn't thought of her."

So they tried — held another meeting, with Mrs. Russell present, put all the conditions before her. She asked for time to decide and left them.

I received the report of the meeting. A strange peace came into my heart. I had met Mrs. Russell in Florida, and had been very favorably impressed by her sincerity and frankness. I felt encouraged.

Some time after this, I made a lecture in one of our great cities. After the lecture, I went to the Hotel and retired. But I could not sleep. I was thinking of the little, struggling School in the Cumberlands—the School which represented the sum total of my life's work. Suddenly, a thought came to me. I got up and wrote a letter to Mrs. Russell. She got the letter just a few hours before the time set for her decision, and decided that she would accept.

She came to us in April, 1922. I had several talks with her, then went back to my lectures for the Bureaus, leaving the administration in her hands.

From the very first, she began to succeed. She put everything on a strictly business basis. She won the respect and confidence of all. She was lavish in her personal gifts to students and to the poor and needy. But she conserved every penny of the School's money and made it count to the utmost. She inspired the students. She held before them the highest ideals of personal character and attainment. She loaned them money— her own money. She paid many of the School's debts, out of her own pocket. She was silent, retiring, but a tremendous force. I have never seen such a wonder.

In less than two years every dollar of the thirty-two thousand had been paid promptly and running expenses had been met. How my heart rejoiced as I went about my work!

Gymnasium

MELROSE HALL

Melrose Hall—A dormitory for girls.

CHAPTER XXII.

In the Summer of 1923, when we had freed our school from debt, a challenge to bigger things came, as usual, from a most unexpected source.

M. C. Treat, of Pasadena, Calif., offered us fifty thousand dollars to be used in building a dormitory for girls if we would raise a like amount for other buildings. He also suggested that I come to California to raise my fifty thousand.

This was the biggest thing which had come to us. If it could be accomplished it would mean success for Oneida Institute.

But I was tired and unwell. Constant toil and continuous anxiety for more than a quarter of a century had nearly exhausted the springs of life. I halted, hesitated, faltered.

Could it be done? Was it humanly possible? We had just appealed to our friends to pay a debt of thirty-two thousand dollars, and they had done it. Would they respond to this appeal for fifty thousand more? Could I stand the strain of it? Yes, I could and would. I might fall, but I would fall at my post. I would make the attempt and trust in Him who watched over us while we built our first house and slept on pillows of shavings.

So I arranged with the Ellison-White Lyceum Bu-

Milo C. Treat.

reau to give me a few lecture dates, en route, to pay traveling expenses. When I reached Los Angeles I had less than óne hundred dollars. I secured a dingy little room for seven dollars per week and tried to keep my eating expenses down to one dollar per day.

Through the friendship of Mr. Coit, President of the Coit-Alber Lyceum Bureau of Cleveland, Ohio, I was given an opportunity to make many lectures in Los Angeles and vicinity. What time I wasn't lecturing I was talking to individuals. I kept this up for five weeks, but people were slow to act. I tried to put my very soul into every effort. The people seemed intensely interested, but still no move was made.

Time dragged on from day to day—another attempt and another disappointment. My exchequer was almost depleted—my heart was sore. Then something happened. Bob Carnahan came from his home in Pine Bluff, Ark. He took me to the Rosslyn Hotel, got me a room with bath, paid all the eating bills, bought me a new suit of clothes, hired an auto and took me to every engagement.

We kept this up for six weeks longer, and, at the last Bob gave a banquet at which we raised four thousand dollars. We still lacked ten thousand dollars of the goal. Bob pledged five thousand dollars and underwrote my pledge for five thousand. This ended the drive. We succeeded.

But here is a strange thing. Considerably less than half of the fifty thousand we raised came from my strenuous efforts on the Pacific Coast. Mrs. Russell kept the office force at Oneida busy. Every mail took scores of letters to our friends, and they responded nobly. The records show that more than thirteen hundred people contributed to the fund of fifty thousand dollars. Out of this drive has come Melrose Hall, an addition to Marvin Hall, the remodeling of Carnahan Hall and a beautiful gymnasium.

In my campaign at Los Angeles I became personally acquainted with M. C. Treat. I visited with him several times. I was surprised at the simplicity of the man and his home. I didn't talk much, I listened to him. There was nothing else to do. He was a man of giant intellect. His first thought was the cause for which our Savior died. That was of more importance to him than everything else in this world. All the treasures of this world should be laid at the feet of the Man of Calvary. What an inspiration it is to have known a man of such sterling worth! He was shy of publicity. He prayed in his closet. I think he was the most positive personal power with which I have ever come in contact—in some peculiar sense the biggest man it has ever been my fortune to know.

SUMMARY.

This little book is made up of excerpts from the annals of my soul. It is the laying bare of heart experiences. It is not an autobiography. It portrays only a certain phase of my life—only one phase.

I shrank from the very thought of making these experiences public. It was at the insistent importuning of hundreds of friends that I, after many years, consented to write.

In writing these memoirs, I have tried to be frank and honest. There is nothing dogmatic in this book. The philosophy of events, herein expressed, is my own. I do not ask any one to accept my interpretations.

From first to last, I have been a rebel—always rebellious. In my mind, I have resigned as president of Oneida Institute thousands of times. I have spent many lonely, tear-stained sessions with Elijah in the wilderness. I have, many times, been so completely discouraged, that I did not even dare to think. I have sought refuge from overwhelming cares and anxieties in games, often till after the midnight hour, just as a respite from thinking. I do not suppose that the good pals who played Tennis, Forty-two, and Dixie Rook with me ever even dreamed that they were bringing surcease to an overburdened heart.

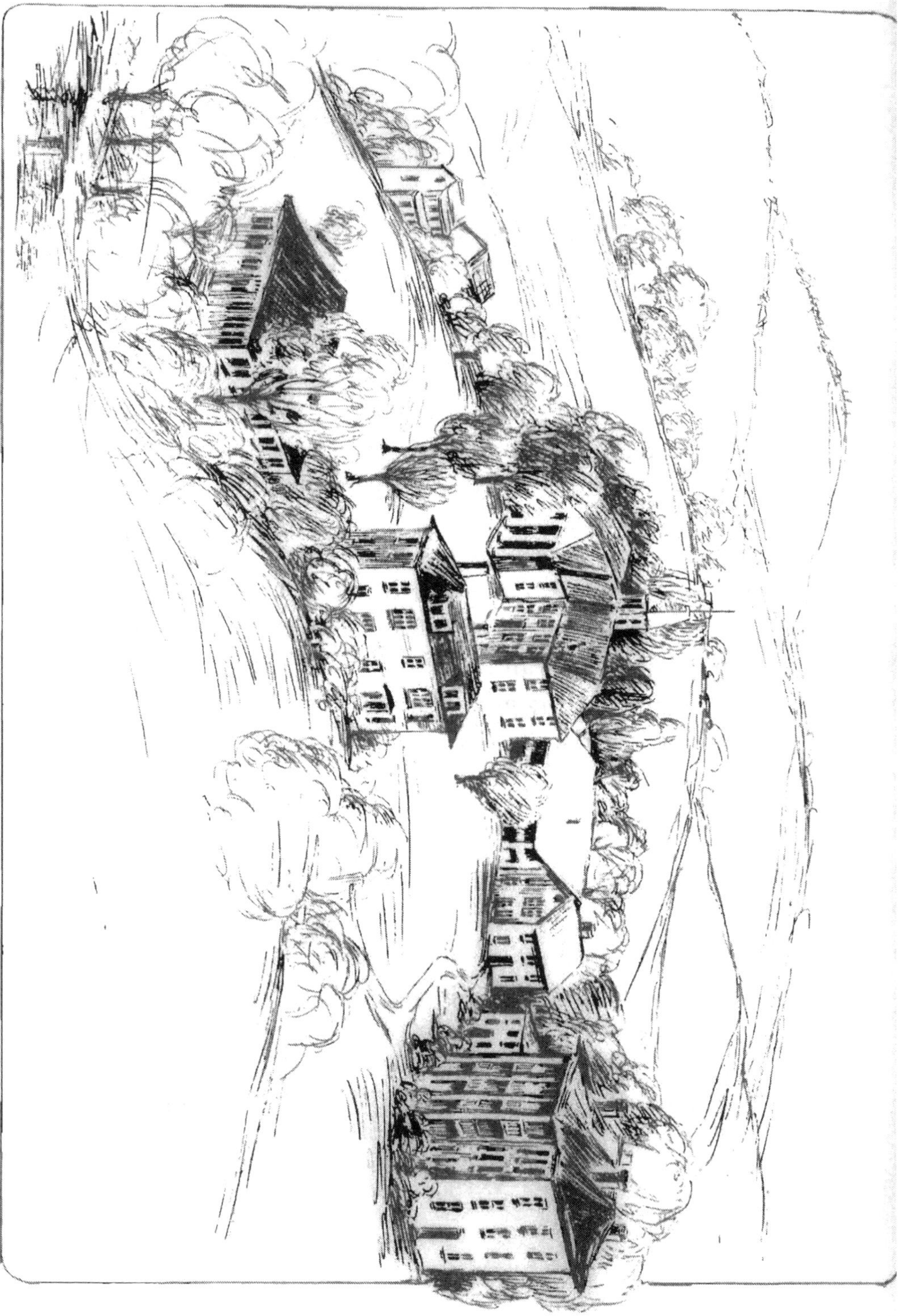

But, through the distracting cross-currents of life, I have been piloted safely.

> "Sometimes 'mid scenes of deepest gloom—
> Sometimes where Eden's bowers bloom—
> By waters still, o'er troubled sea—
> Still 'tis God's hand that leadeth me."

I have lived to see our mountain children emancipated from the bondage of illiteracy and freed from the blight of the feud spirit. I have seen the smoky log-cabin replaced by the beautiful white cottage. I have heard the vengeful barking of the Winchester grow fainter and fainter and finally die away in the silence of peace. We taught the children to love and respect each other and the feuds died a natural death—automatically. Peace can never be secured by drastic laws, battleships, and big guns. But when the children of this world are taught to love each other, then strife and rapine will cease.

Finally, I want to disclaim any glory whatever for the work of Oneida Institute. I did not choose this work. I was chosen for it by Him who works in us both to *will* and to *do* of His good pleasure. It was impinged upon me—the only job I ever had. It has grown from the vaguest kind of a vision to an Institution with property worth half a million dollars. It has trained hundreds of faithful teachers who have carried the message of peace to thousands of helpless children in the fastnesses of the Cumberlands. The realization of this is ample remuneration for every day of toil and every night of privation.

Throughout the years I have been surrounded by a host of noble souls—faithful co-laborers at Oneida, and faithful benefactors scattered far and wide—friends of humanity whose names are written in the Book of Life. I have done my part of the work, and they have done theirs. If I labored more abundantly, it was really not I, but the grace of God which was with me.

There will be a sequel to this book—maybe more than one. If I do not write it, someone else will. The work of Oneida Institute has scarcely begun. It shall be carried on into the ages, a heritage for generations yet unborn. Workers will live and love and labor till their tasks are done—others will rise up to take their places—to carry the banner still further to the front—whither, we do not know. But when the end has come, and the sheaves are garnered, we'll cast our trophies at His feet.

Dr. Preston Jennings Jones.

DR. PRESTON JENNINGS JONES

For the last twenty years this wonderful physician has served Oneida Institute without money and without price, voluntarily and gratuitously. He has been the good Samaritan of Oneida with a radius of twenty-five miles. He has ridden day and night at any call, winter and summer, averaging at least four thousand miles a year. He has served the poor people just as faithfully as those who were able to pay for service. He is perhaps the most influential, as well as the best loved man, in the mountains of Kentucky.

R. Carnahan, Jr.

First treasurer of Oneida Institute. He is the man who really kept the school alive in its early struggles. The over-drafts which he paid were sometimes as much as fifteen thousand dollars. He was born and reared in a log cabin near Manchester, Ky. His first job was a clerkship in a little store for which he received eight dollars per month. He then got into the lumber business and is now one of the leading lumber men of our nation.

A POSTLUDE

THERE comes to me the recollection of a legend I have heard sometime, somewhere—that if a living being be shut up in the walls of a building, the building will have a soul. So here, the life-blood of the man seems to speak out from each brick and stone in these buildings and from every blade of grass, from every twig and from every tree.

A visitor to the Institute, eminently successful in the world of business, after thorough investigation of the school, most sagely remarked: "Oneida Institute would never have existed, if it had depended upon a business man to build it, for a business man would have known it could not be done. It took a dreamer and a man of vision to make it possible."

There is that intangible, indescribable, inexpressible something which pervades this Institution—something not to be found in any other. We marvel at the man; we wonder at the work, which he, through God, has wrought.

Standing today—a living monument to one man's simple faith in God and confidence in humanity—is *Oneida Institute*.

MRS. SYLVIA W. RUSSELL
President-Associate

Printed in the USA
CPSIA information can be obtained
at www.ICGtesting.com
LVHW011725241223
767353LV00017B/1242